DAD How Does Money Work???

Volume 1

by

Sly Fleming, MBA, CCLC

Co-Authored Isaiah & Samuel Fleming

HERITANCE CHANGERS Publishing

Changing your Paradigms

3611 Mt. Holly-Huntersville. Rd # 218 Charlotte, NC 28216

Dad, How Does Money Work
Volume 1

Published by: Inheritance Changers, Inc
3611 Mt. Holly-Huntersville Rd. Suite 218
Charlotte, NC 28216

Edited by: Laura Jackson

Unless otherwise stated, all scripture references are taken from the New International Version(NIV) of the Bible.

ISBN 978-1-937353-06-3

Printed in the United States of America

CONTENTS

Volume 1

FORWARD

For years I worked as a financial advisor representing one of the largest financial firms in the world. As I worked with my clients, I often would hear my clients say, “If I would have known this when I was younger, I would have ....” They spoke with regret about the costly mistakes they would have avoided and the investments they would have made if they would have had more knowledge about money.

Understanding money is important in our society, yet we live each day knowing little about it. What is even more disheartening is how little we teach our youth about money and its uses. What type of future could our middle school or high school students have if they began to understand money while still living at home with no bills or responsibilities? What type of life could they build with a strong financial foundation?

We wrote this series of books for beginners, so the age of the reader really doesn't matter. If you need to learn more about finances or you want to build a strong financial foundation, this series is for you.

To keep the attention of our financial beginners, we separated the subject matter into volumes. This will allow you to focus on certain topics while avoiding information overload. Inside you'll find a blend of history, logic and application. This format will help you get a full well rounded understanding of money and its functions.

This book is your starting point but by no means should it be the end of your financial journey. If you continue to take one step at a time, you'll gain an understanding of money that you can teach your children and future generations.

Sly Fleming

Volume 1

Dad, How Does Money Work ?

Introduction

If you're a financial beginner, I wrote this book especially for you. Let me tell you a secret: Most of our parents never truly gained a proper understanding of money and finance. They developed what we call a working knowledge of finance and money over the years. A working knowledge is another way of saying that they have enough understanding to get through the basic functions of money and finance. Sadly, however, some individuals never develop a good grasp of these concepts.

With that fact in mind, I wrote this book to help any who wants to develop a functional financial foundation. Or just maybe you can use it as a tool to teach someone else. You see, I have three sons of my own, and I want them to have a better financial start in life than I had. They will help me write this book so I can present the information in a way that a young novice can understand it.

Every chapter is based on a question that one of my sons had asked me about a foundational concept of money. In order to answer the question in a way that it will be useful, I will explain the concept and give examples and takeaways so that you will understand different aspects of money.

In this book, my sons and I will teach you things that your parents may or may not have taught you. All parents aren't ready to teach you what you're about to learn in this book series. Don't blame them; after all, they can't teach you if they never learned this information.

You've just entered into the realm of becoming an **Inheritance Changer**. You may ask, "What does this mean?" Think about it, If you do something positive to change your life, that change will not only affect your life but also the lives of your family, your friends and your future generations. By reading this book, you're about to change your understanding of money. This in turn will affect the very way that you prepare and respond in certain situations of life. In turn becoming an Inheritance Changer because you are changing the Inheritance of your future generations.

Are you ready for the challenge? Are you ready to be the person everyone looks to for answers about money (maybe even your parents one day)? If so, let's begin. This will be a book that you can refer to for guidance or keep to pass on to your own children one day. For now, enjoy it, because it's all about you.

Congratulations on becoming an **Inheritance Changer**! Nothing can stand in your way or stop you from having the future that you want as long as you continue to move towards it.

Volume 1

CHAPTER 1

WHAT IS THE DIFFERENCE BETWEEN BEING RICH AND BEING WEALTHY?

What is the difference between being rich and being wealthy?

This question is a foundational piece of understanding when it comes to your own ability to grow wealth and prosper. You could ask this question to 10 different people, and depending on their backgrounds, their beliefs, and other variables you could get 10 different answers. In order not to get too complicated, let's first look at what Webster's Dictionary has to say about it.

Rich:

> Is having wealth or great possessions; abundantly supplied with resources, means, or funds; wealthy: a rich man; a rich nation

Also according to Webster's Dictionary is the definition of wealth:

Wealth:

1. a great quantity or store of money, valuable possessions, property, or other riches: the wealth of a city.

2. an abundance or profusion of anything; plentiful amount: a wealth of imagery.

3. Economics.

   a. all things that have a monetary or exchange value.

   b. anything that has utility and is capable of being appropriated or exchanged.

4. rich or valuable contents or produce: the wealth of the soil.

5. the state of being rich; prosperity; affluence: persons of wealth and standing.

Now that we know what Webster has to say about these terms, let us get into some practical definitions. Son, people often use these two words interchangeably, but in actuality they are quite different, at least for your teaching today. A person can be wealthy, but not rich. On the other hand, it's almost impossible to be rich and not wealthy. When talking about wealth, Webster's definition, in my perspective, is pretty close with its meaning; however, we'll clean it up a bit for our purposes.

Wealth: (Inheritance Changer's (IC) definition

Wealth is the possession of something in abundance that is tradable and holds value in a way that can be used as currency. This means we can value and measure it.

In the ancient days, people sometimes used sheep, cattle, goats and gold to measure wealth. These items still hold value today. We also measure our wealth today in dollars, property, investments and other items. With this in mind, you must understand how to measure your wealth and how people define it in the time and place that you live.

In the account of Esau and Jacob in the Old Testament of the Bible, Esau sold his birthright to Jacob for a bowl of stew (see Genesis 25: 29-34). Esau put an enormous amount of value on the bowl of stew that his brother Jacob prepared. In retrospect, Esau discovered that he had assigned too much value to it, but when he thought he was going to starve to death, giving up his birthright for a bowl of stew seemed like a fair trade.

This story brings up some key elements that we will talk about later such as **supply and demand, time value, and need-based value**. To keep others from cheating or taking advantage of you, you must have a measuring system that works regardless of your personal emotions. This will help you give a clear picture of wealth to any item or service. Note to self, remember, that most individuals who find themselves being manipulated in a transfer of wealth do so because of their own emotions playing a part of the decision making process.

POINT OF CLARITY

Transfer of wealth is the purchase, sell, or the giving of anything of value. The item is normally not consumable like a meal or buying gas.

In the world today, we have trade values on currency; for instance dollars (which is the American form of currency) versus Euro (which is the European form of currency). This measuring system is everywhere. Think how much a burger is worth at a local fast-food restaurant. Now how much is it worth to you when you're hungry? The price remains the same but the value doesn't. Similarly, gas prices fluctuate depending on demand.

Being wealthy comes down to looking at what you're accumulating and answering a fundamental question: Is this item adding value to your wealth or taking value away from your wealth? Keep this simple equation in mind when thinking about wealth:

Wealth = Assets - Liabilities - Expenses

Without proper explanation of this equation some may say that this book just got real -- or shall I say real complicated. Relax, we're taking this slow. Before we can truly define wealth we must first understand the other members of this equation.

First, what is an asset?

Wealth: (Inheritance Changer's (IC) definition

An asset is something that when purchased or acquired, it has a value or re-sale value. Meaning if I had to sell it, it would be equal to a certain monetary value or in simple terms a dollar amount.

POINT OF CLARITY

Monetary Value - just means, how much money is it worth?

Next, What is an Liability ?

Liability: (Inheritance Changer's (IC) definition

A liability is in short something that you are trying to pay off such as a loan for a car or a mortgage for a home. There are many types and categories of liabilities; we will go further into the concepts of liabilities later. This definition is merely for you to help identify your wealth.

POINT OF CLARITY

We often refer to liabilities as debt, b that you have payments on, or peop you may owe.

Normally it really means paying off wl you owe on an asset.

Finally, what are expenses?

Expenses: (Inheritance Changer's (IC) definition

Expenses are the things that we pay to maintain a household or enjoy a standard of living. Some expenses, such as paying light bills, are necessities. Some, like going out to eat, are luxuries. Sometimes these "luxuries" can become habit forming and increase your expenses.

POINT OF CLARITY

Normally you can identify an expense by it being a payment for a service or a bill that covers time; such as a rental.

Now that we've defined our equation, let's take a step back and ask what would a wealthy person consider wealth accumulation.

POINT OF CLARITY

Wealth accumulation means the gathering of wealth or assets.

To grasp this concept about wealth, let's identify an item. We'll determine if it is the accumulation of wealth or if it is an illusion of wealth accumulation.

First Item: Clothing

Step 1: Is the item a product or a service?

In this case clothing is a product, unlike renting a tuxedo. If it were a rented tuxedo, it wouldn't qualify as an asset because you would have to return it. Because you're making a purchase, this item of clothing does start out as an asset.

Step 2: Does this asset carry any liabilities with it?

Do you truly own this asset? Did you purchase the item of clothing on a credit card, if so, then the bill on the credit card to cover this purchase would be a liability.

Step 3: Does this asset create any expenses. For instance, do you have to take the item to the cleaners, like a uniform that requires weekly cleaning for work? Or can this item be washed at home?

Step 4: Does your item have monetary value? If so, how much? You can also consider monetary value as resale value. This is the current value of your asset.

Wealth = Assets - Liabilities - Expenses

After you complete these four steps, use your equation. If the final number is a positive number, then it is adding to your wealth.

Now that we've examined the definition of wealth, what does being rich entail? Being rich is:

Rich : (Inheritance Changer's (IC) definition

Being rich means so much more than just having material wealth. It is a way of life. To be rich is the accumulation of all things. This in itself gives a priceless status of life, which we know of as being rich.

POINT OF CLARITY

Being rich is more than material items, it is a accumulation of all aspects of life.

The confusing part about being rich is that it is self-defining. Indeed, being rich has become so interchangeable with wealth that we have lost its true definition. What makes a person rich is his or her health, family, morals, lifestyle and fulfillment in life along with his or her wealth.

To be rich, you must take a self-evaluation of all parts that add up to the classification of being rich and then give your judgment using your own measuring stick.

Son, when I was your age a man once ask me, did I want to be rich. People typically answer this question with a loud and resounding YES. This man asked me again. I guess he didn't hear my scream the first time, so I yelled "YES" twice as loud, thinking that if he heard the word longer and louder he would feel compelled to reach in his pocket and give me the money to start me on my way to being filthy rich.

As if he didn't hear me screaming at the top of my lungs, he continued to ask me one last time: Do you want to be rich? This time I felt that his hearing aid must not be working right so I just said yes, in a soft voice, while making large mouth movements, hoping that if he couldn't hear me at least he could read my lips.

This time after I answered he smiled at me and asked me to come closer. I thought, "This is going to be my big payoff, and I can buy my mama the house she's been wanting." I came closer, expecting my reward for giving this man such a firm, deliberate answer. Instead this man looked me in the eye and said, “Riches aren’t silver and gold, but may you find sons and daughters, when you grow old, are the true treasures of life.”

I don’t know if he read that phrase somewhere or if he was making it up, but at that moment in my life, his words flew right over my head like a jet plane. Now that I’m older and I have a family of my own, I now understand what he meant. He was telling me that to be rich is the life you live, not the possessions in it.

The purpose of this book is to show you how to be wealthy and rich at the same time. You could just say to be rich. Just think about this: We all know that

Bill Gates is extremely wealthy but only he can define if he is truly rich.

When discussing the ability of being rich or wealthy, one must know its opposite. For instance the opposite of wealthy is poverty and the opposite of rich is poor. Let's see what Webster's has to say:

Poverty:

1. the state or condition of having little or no money, goods, or means of support; condition of being poor; indigence

Poor:

having little or no money, goods, or other means of support: a poor family living on welfare.

Now that we know the world's view, let's look at the IC Definitions:

Poverty: (Inheritance Changer's (IC) definition

Poverty is the lack possessions or something that is tradable and holds value in a way that can be used as currency. This means that you can measure and value the item.

Poor: (Inheritance Changer's (IC) definition

To be poor is so much more than just the lack of material wealth, it is a way of life. To be poor is the accumulation of all things in life to give a status of being poor, for example a poor mentality.

Just remember: You can be rich and still live in poverty, but if you're poor it's only a matter of time until poverty finds you.

Now that we know the difference between being rich and being wealthy, being poor and living in poverty: let us start the fun part. As a young adult you still living have the ability to dream big and to go after your dreams. Armed with the definition and understanding of wealth, how much do you want to accumulate before you leave your parents' home? What is your definition of rich in your own words? Write down your goals and then put them in a place where you can be reminded of them daily and let nothing stand in your way.

Review

1. **If you're wealthy, you must be rich (T/F)**

2. **In order to understand wealth, it must be measurable (T/F)**

3. **A family in poverty cannot be rich (T/F)**

4. **A wealthy family can be poor (T/F)**

5. **Rich and poor are ways of life (T/F)**

6. **If a person has $1 million, we might consider that person:**
    a. **Poor**
    b. **Rich**
    c. **Poverty**
    d. **Wealthy**

7. **If the same person has $1 million, good health, a positive mentality, nice family, and no stress, this person might consider himself**
    a. **Poor**
    b. **Rich**
    c. **Poverty**
    d. **Wealthy**
    e. **A and B**
    f. **B and D**

8. **If another family had everything from above except the $1million, those family members might classify themselves**
    a. **Poor**
    b. **Rich**
    c. **Poverty**
    d. **Wealthy**
    e. **A and C**
    f. **B and C**

Scripture Readings

Passage Romans 12:2: (Young's Literal Translation(YLT))

[2]and be not conformed to this age, but be transformed by the renewing of your mind, for your proving what [is] the will of God -- the good, and acceptable, and perfect.

Passage Proverbs 1:5: (The Amplified)
[5]The wise also will hear and increase in learning, and the person of understanding will acquire skill and attain to sound counsel [so that he may be able to steer his course rightly]--

Passage Proverbs 4:7: (YLT)

[7]The first thing [is] wisdom -- get wisdom, And with all thy getting get understanding.

Passage Proverbs 10:4: (YLT)

4Poor [is] he who is working -- a slothful hand, And the hand of the diligent maketh rich.

Passage Proverbs 10:15 (YLT)

15The wealth of the rich [is] his strong city, The ruin of the poor [is] their poverty.

Passage Proverbs 22:1-2: (English Standard Version (ESV))

1 A good name is to be chosen rather than great riches,
and favor is better than silver or gold.
2 The rich and the poor meet together;
the LORD is the maker of them all.

Passage Proverbs 22:6-7: (ESV)

6 Train up a child in the way he should go;
even when he is old he will not depart from it.
7 The rich rules over the poor,
and the borrower is the slave of the lender.

To Do

1. What will make you rich? Write your thoughts below.

2. Please write down what your own personal goals of wealth.

CHAPTER 2

DAD, WHAT IS MONEY AND HOW DOES IT WORKS?

Dad, What is money and how does it work?

This is a great question. We could spend all day talking about this subject. Most individuals spend the majority of their lives not really understanding money and how it works. For this reason alone money can potentially have power over its user.

The Bible states, "The love of money is the root of all evil." (See 1 Timothy 6:10) This is probably because money is a tool, not something we should love. You'd never find a person truly in love with a hammer, so why should money be any different? If truth be told, money is a make-believe entity to which we've given power. For the purposes of this chapter we'll go into the more traditional understanding of money.

When looking at the different definitions, one definition that could help in this process:

Money: *Any article or substance used as a medium of exchange, measure of wealth, or means of payment, such as checks on demand deposit. The purpose of money is no more than a means to exchange for goods or services.*

This definition of the word money really doesn't address the totality of what money is and how it works.

For this lesson, let's look at eight ways we have misused money. Then we can identify it and see how it can work for you.

1. **People use money to establish power.**

   We've all seen individuals or organizations who, because of their money, may feel that they're above the law or they may have their own set of rules.

POINT OF CLARITY

This is that person who says, "You can't do that to me. Do you know who I am?"

2. **We use money to establish class systems or to gain status among our peers.**

    a. A class system means that because people may be wealthy, they get special privileges. Further, others may look down on them for spending time with those who lives in poverty.

    b. Have you ever seen people refuse to hang out with those who aren't as wealthy or well off as they are? (Some adults still do this. They buy homes they can't afford just to feel like they belong.) This is keeping up with the Jones.

POINT OF CLARITY

This person may say, " I don't hang out with broke folk"

3. **We use money to buy other's affection.**

   a. Have you ever met someone who believed he/she had to buy people things to get them to like them? (Some professional athletes and actors also fall in this category.)

b. Some men will even try to buy the affection of a lady that they might like (Don't be surprised but women do it too).

POINT OF CLARITY

This might be the guy who goes in a club and tries to make it rain . ("Making it rain" means to throw money up in the air and let it fall to the floor, just for the attention)

4. **We bribe people with money.**

    a. Some people try to get others to do things they normally wouldn't for the promise of money.

POINT OF CLARITY

Come on, if you go with me I will pay your way

5. **We use money to buy happiness.**

    a. There are some individuals who believe that they don't need true friends because they have money. What happens when the money is gone?

POINT OF CLARITY

I just have to have the best and most expensive of everything to survive.

Those without true friends and money find themselves attracting a type of acquaintance known a a gold digger

A gold digger according to Webster's is: Informal. A woman who associates with or marries a man chiefly for material gain.

Now that we're in the 21st century, gold diggers have evolved into so much more. They're men and women who hang around to get access to someone else's money. You might know them as groupies, leeches, chicken heads and so much more. I just call them fake friends because they care more about your money than they do about you. Most of the times there true colors won't present itself until it is too late.

6. **Some people get their identity and sense of self-worth from money.**

    a. If needed, go back to chapter one to understand the difference between being rich and being wealthy.

POINT OF CLARITY

These people validate who they are by their bank accounts or job titles.

7. **We use money as a motivator**

    a. Using money as a motivator isn't necessarily bad. For example, men and women go to work every day to earn a paycheck.

    b. The real issue is this: What are you asking someone to do for money? If you offer someone $500 to do something wrong or illegal, then you're misusing money.

    c. Remember money is a tool designed for work. When it becomes the object of your desire, you're in trouble.

POINT OF CLARITY

These people love to see their friends compete for their money. Or they involve themselves in the ultimate money chase.

8. **For some people, money has become everything.**

    a. 1 Timothy 6:10

    b. For a root of all the evils is the love of money, which certain longing for did go astray from the faith, and themselves did pierce through with many sorrows;

(Young's Literal Translation)

POINT OF CLARITY

This person can't think about anything else other than making or having money.

Now that we know some of the things that money can't do, let's dig deeper and find out a little more about what money can do. First let's address this quote: "Money can't buy you happiness." That's not entirely true. It's depends on what makes you happy. The individuals who use this phrase try to make money an identifier, and that is not money's purpose.

Money is more of an amplifier, meaning that if you're a mean person without money, you'll probably be really mean with it. The same hold true about niceness. So think about the things you love doing now without money, and you may be able to do them better, longer, and at a different level with money.

The reason this holds true is because money is a form of exchange. You buy the very things you want using money as an exchange for a good or service. Goods include food, toys, clothing, and much more.

Services could be after school care, a football game, a trip to the barber, a night out, and so on.

Just remember, money is a tool to do things. If you were going to dig a hole, for example, you might use a shovel. You wouldn't fall in love with your shovel but it would allow you to dig a hole, and the bigger your shovel the quicker you can dig this hole. Think about this: If you loved your shovel and you had to dig a hole, you might not dig in the dirt for fear that your shovel might break. Or if someone needed to borrow your shovel, you might say no because you would focus more on the shovel than the hole that needed to be dug.

Hence the phrase "the love of money is the root of all evil". This also opens another question: If I'm in love with money, when is enough, enough? Now you've created a chase for a never-ending goal.

Before we move forward, let's do a brief history of the concept or today's idea of money. Most of the money that we value and we know about our society has no intrinsic value of its own. That means money is now a fiat currency or a decreed currency.

POINT OF CLARITY

Fiat or decreed just means that we say it is good. In other words, it's stated money.

We used to back up our money with precious metals. During this time we called it a commodity currency. However, before there was money as we know it today, individuals often used other items as forms of payment. In ancient Rome, for example, soldiers would sometimes receive bags of salt for their labor. The Latin word for salt is sal, which is the root of the word salary.

Even before people used salt, stones, woods, metals and other things for money, people just traded goods and services for goods and services. This was called bartering. A good example of bartering would be trading your baseball cards for maybe a football.

In 1862, the United States issued the first U.S. dollar. During that time people called those dollars greenbacks due to their color and the green ink. In 1862 the U.S. backed those dollars with precious metals. When I was a child, for instance, people told me the government backed our money with the gold in Fort Knox. Our government doesn't use metal to back its money anymore. So how does the dollar holds its value?

Today, money's real value is based on the economic strength of the country that issued it. Therefore, government-issued money is called legal tender, and by law we must accept it as payment. So if a country has a low economic value, the money might not be worth much.

Because money is just a tool, we must understand the different type of monies so that we can properly use them. Because I'm in America, I'll use American currency. If you're in a foreign country, you can use its form of currency. This can happen by using the exchange rate for money. The Exchange Rate is "the ratio at which a unit of the currency of one country can be exchanged for that of another country." For anyone from another country who might be reading this book, remember that the American dollar can increase or decrease in value. This is called appreciating and depreciating. Appreciating means to ncrease in value while depreciating means to decrease n value.

Let’s get to the name of the “tools” or money we use. One is cash which is: money in the form of coins or banknotes issued by a government. Below I have listed the different denominations we use in the United States.

A Penny: is a coin worth one cent
PRESIDENT ABRAHAM LINCOLN (1861-1865)
THE 16TH PRESIDENT

The first penny was minted in 1909 in honor of President Abraham Lincoln's 100th birthday. In 1959 the government changed the back of the coin to capture the Lincoln Memorial.

A **Nickel**: is a coin worth 5 cents

PRESIDENT THOMAS JEFFERSON (1801-1809)

THE 3RD PRESIDENT

ON THE BACK IS MONTICELLO, JEFFERSON'S HOUSE

Made from an alloy 75% Cooper and 25% Nickel

A **Dime**: is a coin worth 10 cents.

PRESIDENT FRANKLIN D. ROOSEVELT (1933-1945)

THE 32ND PRESIDENT

THE ONLY FOUR TERM PRESIDENT

THE BACK OF THE DIME HAS OLIVE BRANCH TO THE LEFT AND AN OAK BRANCH TO THE RIGHT. AND A TORCH IN THE MIDDLE

IT IS MADE OF AN ALLOY THAT CONSIST OF 91.67% COOPER AND 8.33% NICKEL.

IT HAS 118 RIDGES ON ITS OUTSIDE.

THE LATIN WORDS MEAN (OUT OF MANY, ONE)

A **Quarter**: is a coin worth 25 cents.

PRESIDENT GEORGE WASHINGTON (1789-1797)

THE 1ST PRESIDENT

The quarter now has many different backs because there is one for each state

It consists of 91.67 percent copper and 8.33 percent nickel. Before 1965 they were made of silver.

A **Fifty Cent Piece**: is a coin that is worth 50 cents.

PRESIDENT JOHN F. KENNEDY (1961-1963)

THE 35TH PRESIDENT

A **Gold Dollar**: is a coin worth 100 cents.
Sacagawea was the teenage Shoshone Indian who assisted the historic Lewis and Clark expedition.

A **Dollar Bill:** is worth 100 cents.
PRESIDENT GEORGE WASHINGTON (1789-1797)
THE 1ST PRESIDENT

The American dollar is one of the backbones of our society. The dollar has some very distinctive markings in order to have a very specific identity.

First let's look at the letter B with the seal around it. This identifies which Federal Reserve Bank this bill came from. In this case it is New York. New York, like all states with a Federal Reserve Bank, has a corresponding number. In the case of New York it's th number 2, which is shown in the four corners of the front of this dollar.

Bills also are numbered in two different ways. First they have an eight-digit serial number and the series identification number. Each bill has the signature of the Secretary of the Treasury and the year of its engraving. The value of the bill is noted in all four corners, with President George Washington displayed in the middle.

On the back of the American dollar are two distinct seals and the phrase in "IN GOD WE TRUST." The seal on the left side has a 13-letter Latin motto, ANNUIT COEPTIS, which means, "He has favored our undertaking." The seal includes an all-seeing eye at the apex of the pyramid. At the base of the pyramid is the year of 1776 in Roman numerals. At the bottom is the second motto, NOVUS ORDO SECLORUM, which means, "New order of the ages."

On the seal on the right is the American eagle. The number 13 is prevalent to signify the original 13 state of the union. Count the stars, arrows, stripes, olives leaves, and olives. All have a number of 13.

A **Two Dollar Bill** is worth two dollars.

PRESIDENT THOMAS JEFFERSON (1801-1809)

THE THIRD PRESIDENT

The two dollar bill is the last of the rare bills still in circulation. This bill has never been popular with the public. Thomas Jefferson is the president on the two dollar bill. On the back is an image of the signing of the Declaration of Independence.

A **Five Dollar Bill**: is worth five dollars

President Abraham Lincoln (1861-1865)

THE 16TH PRESIDENT

ON THE BACK IS A PICTURE OF THE LINCOLN MEMORIAL

A **Ten Dollar Bill**: is worth ten dollars.

The United States Secretary of Treasury Alexander Hamilton

Hamilton is the only non-American born individual on American tender. He was born on the West Indian island of Nevis. Because he is on the face of a ten dollar bill, most people think that Hamilton was a president. In fact, he was the first Secretary of Treasury, so he had a lot to do with shaping American monetary policies.

A **Twenty Dollar Bill**: is worth 20 dollars.

PRESIDENT ANDREW JACKSON (1829-1837)

THE 7TH PRESIDENT

ON THE BACK IS A PICTURE OF THE WHITE HOUSE

A **Fifty Dollar Bill**: is worth 50 dollars.

PRESIDENT ULYSSES S. GRANT 1869-1877

THE 18TH PRESIDENT

ON THE BACK IS A PICTURE OF THE CAPITAL

A **Hundred Dollar Bill**: is worth 100 dollars.

Benjamin Franklin

Benjamin Franklin, one of America's founding fathers and greatest citizens, was a creative scientist, a resourceful inventor, a cunning statesman, a thoughtful printer, a deep philosopher and an educated economist. He was born in Boston; however, most people remember the city of Philadelphia as his home.

In 1969, all denominations over the hundred dollar bill were eliminated, so this meant good bye to the following bills.

A **Five Hundred Dollar Bill**: Worth 500 dollars.
PRESIDENT WILLIAM MCKINLEY (1897-1901)
THE 25TH PRESIDENT

A **One Thousand Dollar Bill**: worth 1000 dollars.

PRESIDENT GROVER CLEVELAND (1885-1889, 1893-1897)

THE 22ND & 24TH PRESIDENT

A **Five Thousand Dollar Bill**: worth 5000 dollars.

PRESIDENT JAMES MADISON (1809-1817)

THE 4TH PRESIDENT

A **Ten Thousand Dollar Bill**: worth 10000 dollars

Salmon Portland Chase

Senator and Governor of Ohio, United States

Secretary of Treasury under President Lincoln,

and Chief Justice of the United States.

A **One Hundred Thousand Dollar Bill**: worth 100000 dollars.

PRESIDENT WOODROW WILSON (1913-1921)

THE 28TH PRESIDENT

Now that we've seen the money that's in action and that which the government has eliminated, you might ask: How does it get to me, and what happens when money gets worn out? The answer is that there is a money cycle that the government controls. After money has been created, it goes to the United States Treasury and then to the federal banks. The money then goes to the federal branches and then to the consumer banks, from which we receive the money through money circulation from individuals and businesses.

Money also flows in the reverse, while along the way old and worn currency goes all the way to the U.S. Treasury to be shredded and burned, or if it is a coin, melted down. This is illustrated in figure A below:

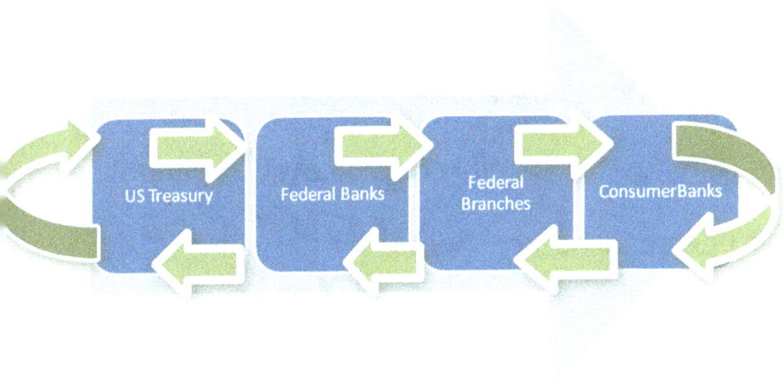

Figure: A

As we said before, there are many forms of money. So what are other forms of money? With the advancement of technology, different avenues are available to the average consumer within the process of moving money. The three areas of money we'll look at are checking, debit and credit cards, and electronic funds transfer.

Checking is the ability to give a promissory note that's backed by the funds in your checking account. This isn't a form of legal tender backed by the government but by your personal funds. Be careful because every organization doesn't personal accept checks.

Figure: B

How do checks work? A check has three major components. First is the routing number on the bottom left of the check. The routing number identifies the bank, its location, the district in which it belongs in the Federal Reserve System and the branch. Now since the check has made it to your bank, next is the account number, which is in the lower middle. The account number verifies that the funds are going in or out of the right person's account.

Last, all checks must have a check number. The check number helps you keep track of the monies going in and out of your account. The number also tells the person receiving the check approximately how long you've had a checking account. The second reason is flawed, however, you can start your check number with any number you want in most cases.

Most checks list your personal information as well as your bank's address and information. This helps the individual who's taking the check feel more assured that they will receive payment on your debt.

How do you write a check? To write a check, first grab a pen. Never sign a legal document with a pencil. You typically want to use a blue or black pen for a legal document. Now let's start with the area entitled "Pay to the order of." This is the person or business entity receiving the check for a good, service or loan.

Next, write the amount in a number format in the box to the right. For example: $20.00. Underneath write out the number in words so that there will be no confusion. For example: Twenty and 00/100 -------------- dollars. The word "and" doesn't appear until you are ready to express the cents. You want to draw a line from the fractional representation of the change to the word dollar so that no one can write anything else. This helps you avoid check fraud.

On the memo line, write what the check is for. This helps you with your record keeping. Last, you must sign your check to make it valid.

To cash a check someone writes to you, you must endorse it, meaning you must sign the back of the check. Most checks identify the space on the back at the top.

If you want to cancel your check, simply write "void" across the front of your check.

POINT OF CLARITY

You can void a check simply by writing the word Void across the front of the check.

We'll briefly examine debit cards and credit cards n this volume. You can use a debit card to access your checking or savings account without going to the bank or writing a check.

POINT OF CLARITY

A savings account is similar to a checking account except its purpose is for saving and the accumulation of wealth.

We'll address credit cards in greater detail later. For now, just remember a credit card gives you access to a line of credit in order to buy something now and pay later with interest.

An EFT or Electronic Funds Transfer typically occurs with a bank or company acting as a middle man. Checks, debit /credit cards and EFT let you access large amounts of money without carrying an enormous amount of cash with you.

Remember money is nothing more than a means for exchanging goods or services through an object that we have given an inherent value (i.e. cash, check, credit, or etc). Without the value that we give to money it wouldn't have any worth, so the next time you want a lot of money, ask yourself what goods or services you're trying to acquire.

Money also helps us keep track of the worth of goods and services. In short, money is our way of keeping order in our financial lives.

Review

What is the purpose of money?

What is legal tender, and what are their forms?

What is an exchange rate?

What major event happened in 1969?

What is the flow of money?

What's so special about Alexander Hamilton?

What major event happened in 1965?

To Do:

Today is a great day to go to your local bank and open an account. But before you do, let your local branch manager know this is where you would like to handle your banking business. Find out what makes this particular bank special, and be sure to get the manager's business card.

CHAPTER 3

Dad, What is Interest ?

Dad, What is Interest?

Those who understand interest have it as an eternal employee. Those who don't understand it will live a lifetime as its slave. Some of us are makers of interest while others are takers of interest. Which one do you want to be?

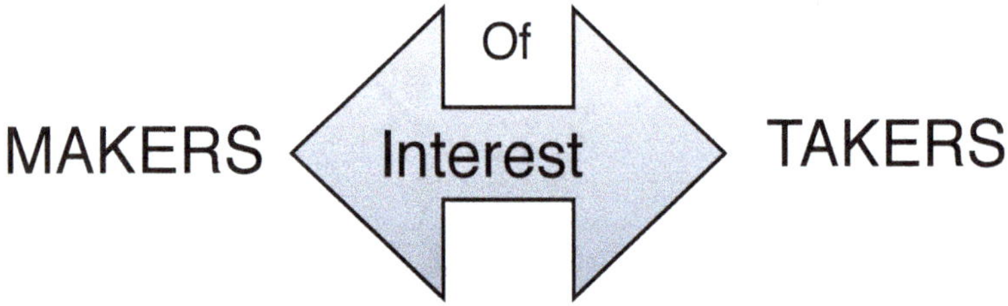

In the Bible, interest is referred to as usury. According to Webster's definition, usury means the lending or the practice of lending money at an exorbitant interest, or interest paid on money.

How can you use the word in its own definition in order to understand the word? You should be leery of such a definition, but this only adds to the mystery of the process that we know as interest.

Interest is an amount of capital or money charged for the borrowing of money. Lenders typically express interest in percentages of the initial monies borrowed. This is now a regulated process due to the practice of loan sharking. Loan sharking is when an individual or business entity charges an amount for the borrowing of money that's above the legal rate.

Depending on where you live, the annual rate for the borrowing of money shouldn't exceed 60 percent annual. This process is highly illegal, which in turn forces most loan sharks to back their loans with threats, violence, the gathering of collateral and criminal behavior. This is probably because they don't have the luxury of having the legal system behind them to collect on bad debts.

POINT OF CLARITY

If the annual rate is above 60% of the initial loan. This is probably Loan Sharking.

We have identified loan sharking as a way to pay interest. Now let's identify some other avenues that we can use to pay interest.

TAKERS/MAKERS OF INTEREST

Personal Loans

In the case of personal loans, a friend, family member or someone you know who has resources will provide money with a fee attached for the use of such funds. This loan normally will have a timetable or specific time by which you must repay the loan. You should discuss the amount of repayment right up front. This loan has either simple interest or a hard dollar amount, which you normally discuss in the initial part of the agreement.

Simple interest is the easiest form of interest to understand and calculate, which makes it a great option for personal loans. The formula for simple interest is below:

I=Interest P = Principle r = Rate t=Time

Interest is the amount paid for the use of the borrowed money.

Principle is the amount borrowed.

Rate is rate of interest being charged for the use of the borrowed money.

Time is the length of time before the loan is completely paid back

Imagine you needed $100 to go to the concert of the year but you didn't have enough money for a ticket. So you asked your Dad for a loan. He agreed to loan you the $100 at 20 percent simple interest, allowing you to pay back the loan with monthly payments for one year.

What would these numbers look like?

The Numbers: if I had a $100 loan at 20 percent interest for one year, my calculations would be as follows:

I=(100)x(.20)x(1) = $20.00 worth of interest.

My total payment would be \$120.00, or \$120 / 12 = \$10.00 per month for a year.

Remember this is only an example. Make some examples of your own. For instance, what would happen if you needed to borrow \$150.00 instead of \$100.00?

Credit Cards

Since the early 1900's, society has toyed with the idea of charge cards or its predecessor the charge plate. But in an effort to not jump off of subject we will table the purpose and use of a credit card until a later chapter. Now, we are looking at how the interest or usury works with a charge card. However, before we move forward lets get an equations together for the purpose of this chapter:

Little Known History Trivia

Charge Account = Credit Card = Charge Plate

Most credit cards make use of a concept known as compounding interest. Compounding interest is when you have a balance of money that's getting a usury charge on a specified timetable. Instead of basing the charge on the initial amount, it's based on the new total each time interest is assessed. In other words, unless you pay more than the interest, the amount you owe will increase.

Let's say you have a credit card compounded monthly at 2 percent for one year. With this knowledge, you buy a computer 500.00 dollars. How much would you have to pay per month to pay it off in two years?

Before we dig deeply into compounding interest, I must first warn you it may take a little time. In fact, most adults don't have a full understanding of how compounding interest works. So first let's look at the equation and then we'll break it down from there.

Complicated MATH

AHEAD

A = Repayment amounts of the Loan

P = The loan amount

i = The interest rate

n = Number of payments

Therefore P=500, i = 2% monthly,

and n= 24 months

$$A=P\left[\frac{i(1+i)^{n}}{(1+i)^{n}-1}\right]$$

I promised not to get too technical and turn this into a math book, so I'll give you the answer. You must pay $26.45 each month to pay off your computer in two years. You would pay $134.80 in interest just for using the charge card. Or you could pay the minimum payment, which would probably be $10.68. If you pay only the minimum, you would pay off the debt in about 15 years. You would spend $1,422.40 in interest payments.

If you don't believe me, ask your parents to go to online and find a compounding interest calculator or a loan calculator. When you plug in the numbers, you'll be amazed at how much you pay in usury.

POINT OF CLARITY

Be careful when dealing with interest,

It can cost you more then you know if

you don't truly understand it.

Mortgages

One of the most confusing forms of interest we'll be talking about is amortization. This word is a version of amortize, which according to Webster's means *to pay off (as a mortgage) gradually usually by periodic payments of principal and interest or by payments to a sinking fund.*

POINT OF CLARITY

According to webster, a sinking fund is a fund set up and accumulated by usually regular deposits for paying off the principal of a debt when it falls due

A little-known fact is that this word comes from the Latin word admortire, which means to kill. I wonder if this was a sick joke when banks started putting mortgages together

Here's another little tidbit of information: The word mortgage also has a Latin origin that means death contract. I wonder how many of your parents would get into a mortgage if they knew they were signing a death contract.

Mortgages, like so many other financial instruments, have evolved over time. When mortgages first started they were a vehicle to help individuals buy a house. I know you're saying, duh! That's what we use them for now.

Did you know that in the beginning, you needed at least 50 percent and sometimes up to 80 percent cash in hand to obtain a three-to five-year loan? Now mortgages average 30 to 40 years, and most people refinance every five to eight years. In case you don't know what refinance means, in layperson's terms it means to reset your mortgage at a different rate.

POINT OF CLARITY

To reset or to refinance your mortgage means just to start over on the time it will take to pay off your loan.

Amortization is the one type of interest that can help you get ahead in your financial life -- if you understand it. On a $200,000 home at 6 percent interest for 30 years, you'll pay more than $430,000 to pay off the loan. We could spend a whole book on this subject alone, but my intent is to introduce the topic and spark a hunger for more knowledge.

Payment Summary

Number of Payments:

360

Monthly Payment:

$1,199.10

Total Principal Paid:

$200,000.00

Total Interest Paid:

$231,676.38

Total Paid:

$431,676.38

From your first payment of $1199.10, only 199.10 goes toward the actual loan amount. Go online and look up amortization tables and make one for yourself so you can see the magic.

Annual versus Monthly Compounding

One of the important things to know when dealing with interest is how often is it compounding. There is a big difference if you pay 6 percent compounding annually versus compounding monthly. This small wording has a lifetime of difference in the amount of interest paid, as shown in the following examples:

Loan Balance:	
	$1,000.00
Loan Interest Rate: Compounding Annual	
	6.00%
Loan Term:	
	1 year
Monthly Loan Payment:	
	$86.07
Number of Payments:	
	12
Cumulative Payments:	
	$1,032.80
Total Interest Paid:	
	$32.80

Note: The monthly loan payment was calculated at 11 payments of $86.07 plus a final payment of $86.03.

Figure 1:

Loan Balance:

$1,000.00

Loan Interest Rate:

Compounding Monthly

6.00%

Loan Term: **1 year**

Monthly Loan Payment:

$119.28

Number of Payments:

12

Cumulative Payments:

$1,431.31

Total Interest Paid:

$431.31

Note: The monthly loan payment was calculated at 11 payments of $119.28 plus a final payment of $119.23.

WARNING LOAN SHARKING!!!!!

Comes to 72% Annual Interest Rate

Figure 2:

COMPANIES

Most companies wouldn't survive without interest. Productive and profitable companies spend a great deal of their time leveraging and understanding the concepts of interest.

Later in the series we'll discuss amortization, a business form of interest that most individuals use but many don't understand.

The world wants you to believe that amortization is nothing more than just a gradual elimination of a liability or debt such as a mortgage or car, and technically that is true. However, did you know that most of the time you end up paying twice the amount of a purchase that's paid off in a mortgage?

We often refer to amortization as "front-loaded" interest, which means that you'll pay the interest on the loan first before you begin to attack the principal. We'll go deeper into this topic later, so for now I encourage you to study the difference between daily interest and amortized interest. Find out more about simple interest and compounding interest. Learning about these concepts ahead of time will help you beat interest at its own game.

POINT OF CLARITY

According to webster, Leverage is the use of credit to enhance one's speculative capacity in other words you have the advantage.

Review

1. **What is simple interest, and how do I calculate it?**

2. **What is compounding interest, and what is the formula?**

3. **Are you a maker of Interest or a taker of interest?**

4. **What is loan sharking and how can you identify it ?**

5. **What is Amortization?**

6. **What does mortgage mean from its Latin roots?**

Coming up next in

Dad, How Does Money Work?

Volume II: Debt,

In this initial volume of Dad, How Does Money Work, we touched on the subjects of interest, identifying the difference between being rich and being wealthy, we learned a little bit about money. We touched on where and how money originated and some of it uses. However, this is just the beginning of the information that is to come. If you liked the information you received be sure to continue with the rest of our volumes we will begin to go deeper and learn more about the different concepts and strategies behind the mystery of money. Volume two will go into the crazy world we know as debt,. Remember, with this series our goal is to prepare you to get ahead in life when it comes to your finances. So until next time, thank you for your support and keep learning.

WWW.ICUCHANGE.COM

Bibliography

The Guide to Understanding Money & Investing; The Wall Street Journal; 1999 by lightbulb press:Lightbulb Press, 10 Rockefeller Plaza, New York, NY 10020

http://www.enchantedlearning.com

http://www.merriam-webster.com/dictionary

www.ingramcontent.com/pod-product-compliance
Lightning Source LLC
LaVergne TN
LVHW022229200926
848481LV00006B/2192
* 9 7 8 1 9 3 7 3 5 3 0 6 3 *